# BAJAZET

# Jean Racine
# BAJAZET

*Translated by*
*Alan Hollinghurst*

*Introduction by*
*Francis Wyndham*

Chatto & Windus
LONDON

Published in 1991 by
Chatto & Windus Ltd
20 Vauxhall Bridge Road
London SW1V 2SA

All rights reserved. No part of this publication may
be reproduced, stored in a retrieval system or
transmitted in any form, or by any means,
electronic, mechanical, photocopying, recording
or otherwise, without the prior permission of
the publisher.

A CIP catalogue record for this book is available
from the British Library

ISBN 0 7011 3853 X

Copyright © translation by Alan Hollinghurst
1991
Copyright © introduction by Francis Wyndham
1990, 1991

Alan Hollinghurst has asserted his right to be
identified as the translator of this work.

Phototypeset by Intype, London
Printed in Great Britain by
Redwood Press Ltd
Melksham, Wiltshire

# INTRODUCTION

Nobody now pays much attention to the three dramatic uni-
ties of Action, Time and Place. Their legendary attribution
to Aristotle was anyhow incorrect and since his day many
of the greatest playwrights have ignored the last two with
triumphant impunity. Yet I would suggest that the third does
still retain a measure of validity and power, if only because
it reinforces a fundamental limitation peculiar to the experience of 'live theatre'. Actors – and, for that matter, spectators
too – are enclosed within a single, comparatively exiguous
space: the resulting sense of claustrophobic intensity is pro-
foundly linked to the essence of dramatic art, and especially
to that of tragedy. In all Racine's plays this feeling of inescap-
able confinement (both actual and metaphorical) is excitingly
acute – but never more so than in *Bajazet*, where theme and
setting are united to hallucinatory effect. The action unfolds
in a secret, subterranean chamber at the heart of a mysterious
and dangerous maze: the harem within the Sultan's seraglio
at Constantinople – or, as Racine calls it, Byzantium.

Written in 1672, the sixth of his eleven tragedies, this play
is both central to Racine's *oeuvre* and unique in that here
(instead of as usual choosing a subject from ancient Greek,
Roman or Jewish history and myth) he found his inspiration
in an event which had occurred only thirty-seven years pre-
viously: the murder by the Turkish Sultan Murad IV
(Amurat) of his brother Bayezid (Bajazet). Realising that
some excuse for this break with convention was expected of
him, Racine proposed in a famous Second Preface that 'the

remoteness of the country to some extent makes good the excessive closeness of the events in time'. Michel Butor writes in his essay 'Racine and the Gods': 'This singular identification of time with space shows that the Ottoman Empire represents for Racine a sort of modern equivalent to the Roman Empire, and that the fact that the Sultan is the representative of God on earth corresponds to the divine nature of the ancient Emperor.' The point of Butor's essay is that the basic Racinian theme of the pitiless hatred felt by the Gods for humans – whom they force into sin and then punish – applies not only to the pagan deities but also underlies his treatment of the monotheistic religions, whether Jewish (and by extension Christian) or Islamic.

Certainly, the Sultan himself is significantly absent from the scene – away waging an Imperialist war against Babylon (Baghdad) and its Persian ally. But the alternating rumours of his threatened victory and return, or promised defeat and death, control the destinies of those he has left behind with an autarchy as arbitrary as any portents of supernatural intervention.

Bajazet, feared as possibly a popular pretender to the Sultan's throne, has been concealed by his brother Amurat within the harem and unnaturally reared in this airless world of concubines and eunuchs instead of in the active military atmosphere he craves. Roxane, the Sultaness, Amurat's favoured concubine and head of his harem, lusts obsessively after the captive Bajazet, over whom she has power of life and death – and Bajazet feels a tender love, almost like that of a sibling, for his cousin Atalide, who loves him in return. Acomat, the wily Grand Vizier, attempts to manipulate these conflicting passions in order to gain his own political ends. Just as he is the only character not sentimentally involved (apart from a cynical desire to marry Atalide for reasons of state) so is he the only one who can be imagined escaping from the seraglio: he boasts that he knows all its detours but he also knows the way out and we are conscious of his vessels waiting 'where the sea laps at the palace walls . . .' Enclosed in a murky emotional labyrinth as oppressive and tortuous as their physical surroundings – confused and unnerved by the contradictory messages that reach them (often already out of date) from the outside world – the other three are enmeshed ever further in refinements of deceit.

Jules Lemaître called *Bajazet* Racine's most violent and most frightening play. It is also perhaps his most complex, and abounds in ambiguities. For example, in a situation where everyone is condemned to lie, it is the virtuous and self-sacrificing characters (Bajazet and Atalide) who lie most steadily and skilfully, while it can be said for the predatory and brutal Roxane that she at least achieves a rare honesty in her anguished self-analysis. Some of Roxane's speeches show Racine's genius for subtle interpretation of mind and heart at its height – those miraculous passages in which he seems to anticipate and surpass the future successes of bourgeois psychological drama while remaining within the majestic tradition of classical tragedy.

As for Bajazet himself, Lemaître sees him as 'an honest man involved in a false situation, forced to lower himself morally in his own eyes in order to do what he believes to be his duty and to assume an equivocal appearance when he is in reality most heroic'. Another commentator – Roland Barthes – describes him thus: 'A male confined in a female milieu where he is the only man . . . like those geese stuffed for the succulence of their livers, Bajazet is shut up in the dark, preserved and ripened for the pleasure of the Sultaness who will conduct his murder as one controls an orgasm; starting out strongly sexual, one feels him being slowly emasculated by the virile Roxane'. There can seldom have been a more elaborate demonstration of gender reversal on any stage.

The play's two heroines are of equal importance with each

other and its nominal hero. When it was first performed, the role of Atalide was given to Racine's mistress la Champmeslé and for years this character was assumed to be the 'female lead'. But early in the eighteenth century Adrienne Lecouvreur played first Atalide and then (perhaps sensing a shift in public taste) Roxane, and after this the latter became the part to attract great actresses. George Henry Lewes praised Rachel as Roxane: 'She is a born empress ... she carries herself with more queenly grace than any throned monarch.' This is interesting, as other interpretations have emphasised Roxane's origins as a slave. He gives a more specific account of 'her handling of the letter which is brought to her as found upon Atalide and written by Bajazet. She shadowed out the marvellous tampering with the heart, the irritable sophistication of one dreading to be undeceived yet unable to shut her eyes to the horrible fact, crumpling the letter, trying to despise it, yet irresistibly attracted towards it.'

The sensual ferocity of Roxane's nature is more likely to intrigue than to repel a modern sensibility, but Atalide is far from being the type of insipid *larmoyante* victim found so appealing by Racine's contemporaries. On the contrary, it is she who most eloquently expresses Racine's comfortless and pervading belief in the *unfairness* of sin when (although in some ways the most innocent of the participants) she takes upon herself the guilt of them all in an epiphany of Jansenist self-hatred.

Francis Wyndham

# TRANSLATOR'S NOTE

Racine is a famously intractable author to bring into English, in part because his verse-form – alexandrine couplets – has no ready equivalent, in part because the static, concentrated austerity of his neo-classicism is bewilderingly alien to English taste and tradition. Indeed, it is symptomatic of our national hostility to Racine that *Bajazet*, one of his most complex and unusual plays, should have had to wait for its English premi-ère until 1990 – 218 years after it was written. (I discount *The Sultaness*, an adaptation by one Mr Hughes, done in 1717.)

It was clear to me that a translation should aim for the transparency and dignity of the French above all, and that the form should be as natural to British actors as the alexand-rines are to the French: no gimmickry of technique should interpose. Blank verse was the inevitable solution; but though I ~~discounted~~ rhyme (so much heavier in English than in ^decided against^ French, and unavoidably comic in effect) I tried as far as possible to translate couplet for couplet and so to preserve the formal containment of Racine's thought and the architec-ture of his speeches.

There has been an understandable nervous tendency among English translators, raised in the richly metaphorical theatre of Shakespeare and trained to shun repetition as a stylistic fault, to introduce colour and variety into their versions of Racine. I have tried to resist that tendency, and to produce some sort of equivalent to the highly charged and tightly circumscribed vocabulary of the original. I have almost always avoided inversions, and hope, by choosing an idiom which is neither modern nor seventeenth-century pastiche, to have conveyed the clarity as well as the otherness of Racine's seventeenth-century French.

I have also translated the play's two prefaces. The second is of exceptional interest for its vindication of Racine's modern subject in reply to attacks from the camp of Corneille. *Bajazet*, after an initial success, suffered a long decline in popularity, and by the beginning of this century was the least performed of Racine's tragedies. But *Bérénice*, now rightly seen as one of his greatest achievements, was also in eclipse; if *Bajazet* comes to enjoy a new esteem in the English-speaking world, it will be due in large part to Peter Eyre and the cast of the Almeida production; and I am very grateful to them for those occasions when they helped me to a better understanding of the French or to a clearer and more speakable version of the English.

Alan Hollinghurst

Although the subject of this tragedy does not yet appear in any printed history, it is none the less a true story. It is an incident which took place in the harem not more than thirty years ago.[1] Count de Cézy was then ambassador to Constantinople. He was informed of all particulars concerning the death of Bajazet; and there are many people at court who remember having heard him recount them on his return to France. M le Chevalier de Nantouillet is among those people, and it is to him that I am indebted for this history and even for the plan I formed to make it into a tragedy. For this reason I have been obliged to change various details; but since the changes are very slight I see no necessity to explain them to the reader. The main principle to which I held was to change nothing of the morals and customs of the nation; and I took care to suggest nothing which did not conform to the history of the Turks and to the new account of the Ottoman empire, which has been translated from English. Above all I owe much to the advice of M de la Haye,[2] who was good enough to elucidate all the problems that I put to him.

## SECOND PREFACE (1676)

The Sultan Amurat, or Sultan Murad,[3] emperor of the Turks, who took Babylon in 1638, had four brothers. The first, Osman,[4] was emperor before him, and reigned for about three years,[5] at the end of which the janissaries took both his empire and his life. The second was called Orcan. Amurat had him strangled in the first days of his reign.[6] The third was Bajazet, a prince of great promise, and it is he who is the hero of my tragedy. Amurat, whether out of friendship or politics, had spared him until the siege of Babylon. After the taking of that city the victorious Sultan sent to Constantinople an order for his death; and this was borne and executed very much in the manner that I have shown it. Amurat had one further brother, who later became the Sultan Ibrahim, and whom he neglected as a witless prince, who gave him no trouble. The Sultan Mahomet, who reigns today, is the son of that Ibrahim, and so also the nephew of Bajazet.

The details of Bajazet's death do not yet appear in any printed history. Count de Cézy was ambassador to Constantinople at the time of these tragic events in the harem. He was told of the love of Bajazet and of the jealousy of the sultaness; he even on several occasions saw Bajazet, who was sometimes allowed to walk on the headland by the harem, above the Black Sea canal. Count de Cézy described him as a prince of noble bearing. He has since written of the circumstances of his death.[7] And there are still several persons of quality who remember having heard him tell the story after his return to France.

Some readers will be astonished that I have dared put so recent a history on the stage. But I could see nothing in the rules of the dramatic poem to deter me from my undertaking. It is true that I would not advise an author to take so recent

xiii

an event as this as the subject of a tragedy if it had taken place in the country where he wished the tragedy itself to be performed, nor to choose heroes for the theatre who would have been known to most of the audience. Tragic personages must be regarded in a different light from that in which we ordinarily see those whom we have known close to. One could say that the respect we have for heroes increases in proportion to their remoteness from us: *major e longinquo reverentia*.[8] The remoteness of the country to some extent makes good the excessive closeness of the events in time: for if I may say so, people scarcely distinguish between what is a thousand years and what a thousand leagues away from them. Thus it is that Turkish people, for example, however modern they may be, have a dignity upon our stage. One sees them as ancients before their time. Theirs are quite different morals and customs. We have so little commerce with the princes and the other people who inhabit the harem that we consider them as dwellers in another age than our own.

It was very much like this that the Persians were once considered by the Athenians. So the poet Aeschylus finds no difficulty in introducing into a tragedy the mother of Xerxes, who was perhaps still living, or in representing on the Athenian stage the devastation of the Persian court after that prince's downfall. Yet this same Aeschylus had been present in person at the battle of Salamis, where Xerxes had been vanquished. He had also witnessed the defeat of the lieutenants of Darius, Xerxes' father, on the plain of Marathon; for Aeschylus was a man of war, and he was the brother of that famous Cynegeirus so widely spoken of in antiquity, who died so courageously in the attack on one of the king of Persia's vessels.

[9]I have attached great importance to expressing in my tragedy what we know of the morals and wisdom of the Turks. Some people have said that my heroines were too experienced in love and too delicate to be women raised

among people who pass here for barbarians. But, without mentioning all that one reads in travellers' accounts, it seems to me sufficient to point out that the scene is set in the harem. Indeed, is there a court in the world where jealousy and love can be better known than in a place where so many rivals are shut in together, and where all the women have no other study, in their unending idleness, than that of learning to please and to be loved? The men there very probably do not love with the same refinement. So I have taken pains to establish the great difference between the passion of Bajazet and the affections of his lovers. He retains in the midst of his love the ferocity of his nation. And if one finds it strange that he consents to die rather than abandon what he loves and wed that which he does not love, then one has only to read the history of the Turks. One will discover at every turn the contempt that they have for life. One will see in several places to what excess they take their passions, and what simple friendship can make them do: as is evidenced by one of the sons of Suleiman, who killed himself on the corpse of his elder brother, whom he loved dearly, and who had been murdered to assure him of the empire.

1   In fact in 1635
2   Successor to Cézy as ambassador
3   Murad IV, Sultan from September 1623, when he was twenty, until his death on 8 February 1640, who took Baghdad after a siege of more than a month from 15 November to 25 December 1638
4   Osman II
5   1618–22
6   According to Du Verdier's *Summary of the History of the Turks* (1665), which Racine would seem to have read, Orcan and Bajazet were assassinated at the same time
7   In an official report
8   Respect is greater from further off: Tacitus
9   Paragraph in the editions of 1676 and 1687, suppressed in 1697

*Bajazet* was first performed in this translation at the Almeida Theatre, London, on 1 November 1990. The cast was:

| | |
|---|---|
| BAJAZET | Martin Wenner |
| ROXANE | Suzanne Bertish |
| ATALIDE | Olwen Fouéré |
| ACOMAT* | Terence Rigby |
| OSMIN | Oliver Parker |
| ZATIME | Valerie Sarruf |
| ZAIRE | Alison Fielding |
| | |
| Director | Peter Eyre |
| Designer | Chloë Obolensky |
| Lighting | Ben Ormerod |

*at the performances of 26 November to 1 December the part of Acomat was played by Peter Eyre

# LIST OF CHARACTERS

BAJAZET      brother of the Sultan Amurat
ROXANE      Sultaness, favourite of the Sultan
ATALIDE      daughter of the Ottoman line
ACOMAT      Grand Vizier
OSMIN      confidant of the Grand Vizier
ZATIME      slave of the Sultaness
ZAIRE      slave of Atalide

The scene is at Constantinople, formerly called Byzantium, in the royal harem

## ACT ONE, SCENE ONE: *Acomat, Osmin*

ACOMAT

Come, follow me; Roxane will soon be here;
Meanwhile I'll talk to you and hear your news.

OSMIN

But sir, since when have we had access here?
This is a place we never glimpsed before:
Such boldness would have met with instant death.

ACOMAT

When you have been apprised of all that's passed
My presence here will not astonish you.
But, dear Osmin, enough of idle talk.
How anxious I have been for your return!
How glad to see you in Byzantium!
Unfold the secrets that you must have learned
On the long voyage you have made for me.
Give me a true account of what you saw,
Remembering, Osmin, that on your words
The future of the Ottomans depends.
What is the army's mood, and what the king's?

OSMIN

The Babylonians, faithful to their prince,
Saw our surrounding army without fear;

The Persians massed and marched to bring them aid,
And each day brought them nearer to our camp.
There Amurat, tired with the fruitless siege,
Seemed ready to leave Babylon in peace;
Abandoning his powerless assaults,
He waited for the Persians and for war.
But as you know, the journey from the camp
Back to Byzantium is very long;
There were a thousand hazards in my path –
For all my haste, the news I bring is old.

ACOMAT

What part had our brave janissaries in this?
And is their homage to our king sincere?
You must have read the secret of their hearts:
Does Amurat enjoy unchallenged power?

OSMIN

He'd have us think that he is satisfied,
And seemed secure of joyful victory;
But we are not deceived by his false calm:
He feigns a confidence he cannot feel.
His efforts to appease the janissaries
And overcome his fear of them are vain:
He can't disclaim his former enmity
When, seeking to affirm his new-found power,
He plotted to escape their guardianship
And hoped to cut their regiment by half.
I've often given ear to their complaints:
As he still fears them, so they still fear him:
His flatteries have not allayed that hurt.
Your absence is a thing much talked about:
They hanker for the days they still hold dear
When, sure of victory, they fought for you.

ACOMAT

    What, dear Osmin, you think my former glory
    Still lends them courage and lives in their thoughts?
    You think they'd gladly follow me once more
    And know again the voice of their vizier?

OSMIN

    They wait to see the outcome of the war,
    The Sultan's victory or else his flight.
    Though with regret, they answer to his laws,
    The fame of their exploits must be sustained,
    The honour of so many years upheld –
    Although the final outcome rests with fate.
    If Amurat, through their great courage, wins
    The honours of the fields of Babylon
    You'll see them humbled in Byzantium,
    The very types of blind obedience.
    But if in war a sterner destiny
    Rebuffs his growing empire, if he flees,
    Don't doubt that, wild with his disgrace, the men
    Will fuse at once their boldness with their hate,
    Interpreting their loss in battle, sir,
    As heaven's own reprimand to Amurat.
    Meanwhile, if rumours are to be believed,
    He had three months ago dispatched from camp
    A slave charged with some secret ordinance.
    The dumbstruck army feared for Bajazet:
    Trembling lest Amurat, by fierce command,
    Had ordered his own brother's execution.

ACOMAT

    Such was indeed his plan: the slave arrived,
    Disclosed his mission, but found no response.

OSMIN

You don't mean he's returned to Amurat
Without the tribute of his brother's head?

ACOMAT

The slave is dead, Osmin, at my command
Thrown weighted in the deepest Euxine Sea.

OSMIN

But won't the sultan, vexed at this delay,
Be looking for a cause, and for revenge?
How will you answer him?

ACOMAT

                Perhaps by then
I will be troubling him with graver cares.
I know that Amurat has vowed my ruin;
And how he'll welcome me on his return.
You've seen how, to displace me in their hearts,
He's led his men without me to the siege:
He leads the army, while I, in a town,
Am left to exercise a useless power.
What work, and what a place, for a vizier!
But I have used the time more worthily –
I've cultivated fears and doubts for him:
Rumours of these will soon have reached him there.

OSMIN

What have you done?

ACOMAT

                My hope is, Bajazet
Declares himself today – and with Roxane.

OSMIN

    Roxane, sir! whom the sultan chose himself
    From all the beauties that two continents
    Have sent in tribute to adorn his court?
    It's said that she alone has won his love
    And even that Roxane, before she bore
    A son, would be created sultaness.


ACOMAT

    He's done more for her, Osmin, and decreed
    That in his absence she has total power.
    You know the normal harshness of our kings,
    How rarely they will let a brother share
    The dangerous honour of that royal blood
    Which renders him too close in rank to them.
    Half-witted Ibrahim knows no such fear
    And, free from threat, lives an eternal child,
    Equally unfit to live or die,
    The charge of anyone who'll give him food.
    The other, though, a fitter cause for fear,
    Sees Amurat in arms against his life.
    For Bajazet has put away for ever
    The pampered leisure of a sultan's son.
    His childhood over, then he longed for war:
    It was in my command that he first knew
    That noble thrill – you saw him, in the throng,
    Draw after him the love of all the men
    And bloodied taste the glory and the joy
    That a first victory brings to a young heart.
    But cruel Amurat, for all his fears,
    Having no son to guarantee his line,
    Did not yet dare seek vengeance on this brother
    Or risk curtailment of their dynasty.
    Disarmed by this, for some time Amurat
    Kept Bajazet shut up in the harem,

And when he left for battle, warned Roxane
That at the slightest murmur, nothing more,
She, sharing in his hate, sole arbitress,
Must sacrifice the prisoner to his fears.
Left here alone, I felt a righteous rage
Turn all my loyalty to Bajazet.
I hid my plans, but led Roxane to see
The uncertainty of Amurat's return,
Fortunes of war and rumours in the camp;
Defended Bajazet, and stressed his charms,
Which, overshadowed by her jealous cares,
Though plain before her she had never seen.
How did it end? Roxane was overwhelmed
And wanted nothing but to gaze at him.

OSMIN

But how could they elude the jealous watch
Which, like a magic wall, kept them apart?

ACOMAT

Perhaps you will recall the unfounded news
Which reached us here, that Amurat was dead.
On hearing this, Roxane pretended fear
And spread the rumour with a show of grief.
Her tears alarmed her slaves, who thought them real;
The men who guarded Bajazet broke ranks
And when their duty had been bribed away
Their captives in that turmoil dared to meet.
Roxane saw Bajazet and could not hide
From him the order she alone was given.
He's fit for love; he saw his life depend
On pleasing her, and soon, please her he did.
Everything conspired: her care and kindness,
Complicit in the secret she'd revealed,
Sighs all the softer for their being hid,

The silence that they were constrained to keep,
Their rashness, danger and their mutual fears
Had made their hearts and fates for ever one.
And even those who should have found them out
Dared not return to their abandoned charge.

OSMIN

Did Roxane bare her soul to them at once,
And let her passion flare before their eyes?

ACOMAT

No, they know nothing of it; till this day
Her love has been conveyed by Atalide.
Amurat's own father was her uncle
And she was raised together with his sons
And shared with them their father's tenderness.
The prince's vows are made in name to her
But she receives them on Roxane's behalf:
Her only wish is that he love Roxane.
Indeed, Osmin, since they rely on me,
They've promised Atalide shall be my wife.

OSMIN

You love her, sir?

ACOMAT

Do you think at my age
I'd serve the low apprenticeship of love?
And that my time- and effort-hardened heart
Would take the rash advice of vain desire?
Quite other qualities please me in her:
I love in her the blood from which she springs.
Through her I'll be brought close to Bajazet
And so secure myself against his whims.
A vizier always troubles his own masters:

7

No sooner are we chosen than we're feared;
They covet our estates and wish us dead
And in their service none of us grows old.
Today I'm honoured, wooed by Bajazet –
His perils daily reaffirm his love:
But this same Bajazet, once on the throne,
Might well cast off no-longer-needed friends,
And if my loyalty fails to stop his hand
May one day dare to ask for my own head.
I don't know why, Osmin, but I am sure
That – maybe far from now – he'll ask for it.
I serve the sultans faithfully but leave
It to the masses to adore their whims:
I will not trouble with the foolish fad
Of blessing my own death when they announce it.
So that is how I have the entrée here –
And how Roxane at last revealed herself.
Invisible at first, she heard my voice
And dreaded the strict laws of the harem;
But then she banished these confining fears
Which had so compromised our interviews
And chose this secret place where we can meet
And hearts can speak to eyes without constraint.
I'm led here by a slave, through hidden paths,
And . . . Someone's there: Roxane – and Atalide.
Stay, and if need be you can confirm
The weighty news I will relate to her.


ACT ONE, SCENE TWO: *Roxane, Atalide, Zatime,
Zaire, Acomat, Osmin*


ACOMAT

Madam, the truth is as it has been rumoured:
Osmin has seen the sultan and his men.

Vainglorious Amurat still lives in fear,
And still all hearts incline to Bajazet:
In unison they call him to the throne.
Meanwhile the Persians march to Babylon
Beneath whose walls the armies soon must meet
In battle to decide our destinies:
If I have reckoned Osmin's journey right
The outcome is indeed already known:
The sultan flees or triumphs as we talk.
Let's break the silence, madam, speak our will,
And henceforth bar him from Byzantium.
Before we know if he has won or fled
We must pre-empt report, and quickly too.
You've no fear if he flees, and if he triumphs
The firmest purpose is your best resolve:
When the townspeople go to welcome him
You'll be too late to win them from his power.
I know the credulousness of their faith
And how they're curbed by their religion's bit,
And have already schemed for the support
Of the most sacred guardians of our law.
Let Bajazet at last see light again,
Open the palace gates to him, unfurl
Mahomet's fateful standard in his name
Which all will know a sign of gravest need.
The crowd, to whom I've urged the prince's case,
Know only virtue leads him to offend.
A rumour, which I've taken pains to fuel,
Will cause the troubled people to believe
Their sultan spurns them and withdraws forthwith
His court and person from Byzantium.
Let's show the threat he poses Bajazet,
The sentence we were called to execute;
Above all let the prince declare himself
And show those brows so worthy of the crown.

ROXANE

I'm satisfied, and hold to what I promised.
Brave Acomat, go, gather up your friends,
And bring me word of what their feelings are;
I will make a firm response myself
When I've seen Bajazet. Until I know
If our thoughts are as one, I can say nothing.
Go, and return.


ACT ONE, SCENE THREE: *Roxane, Atalide,*
*Zatime, Zaire*


ROXANE

    Atalide, in the end
It's Bajazet who must decide our fate.
We'll have a final meeting: I must know
If he loves me.


ATALIDE

    Have you time to doubt it,
Madam? Hasten to complete your work.
You heard the way the vizier was talking;
You love the prince, but by tomorrow may
No longer hold his freedom in your hands.
Why, even now the furious Amurat
Perhaps comes back to sever his sweet life.
What makes you doubt his love for you today?


ROXANE

Why don't you tell me, since you speak for him?


ATALIDE

Think, madam, of the care he took to please,
What you have done, and what you yet might do,

The risks he's run, his loyalty, and your charms –
Don't all these things speak clearly of his love?
You can be sure your merits fill his thoughts.

ROXANE

I am not sure, and have no peace of mind.
Why won't the wretch, if only to please me,
At least address me as I'd have him do?
A score of times, buoyed up by your accounts,
And revelling in his passion in advance,
I've sought to have assurance of his trust
And had him brought before me secretly.
Excess of love may make me difficult,
Yet – to cut short a barren narrative –
I found no hint of that inflamed distress
That your fond words too richly promised me.
If I'm to give him love and an empire
I shall require more than these vague pledges.

ATALIDE

What further test of love do you propose?

ROXANE

If he loves me, to marry me today.

ATALIDE

O heavens! Marry you! And to what end?

ROXANE

I know it's counter to the sultans' way;
I know they've made themselves a vaunted law
Not to restrain their loves with marriage vows.
Among the beauties jostling for their favour
They sometimes deign to pick a mistress out;
She will be anxious, though, for all her charms:

She goes to meet her master as a slave
And, if she bears a son, still bears that yoke,
Although the law declares her sultaness.
Amurat, nobler, single to this day,
Wanted to give that title to his love:
Gave me the title, gave me power too,
And left me keeper of his brother's life.
But Amurat has never promised me
That he will crown these other gifts with marriage,
And I, who hungered only for that crown,
Have lost all memory of these other gifts.
Why justify myself? It's Bajazet
For whom I have forgotten everything.
Though wretched, the more favoured of the brothers,
He pleased me, though perhaps not seeking to.
My women, guards, the vizier – for him
I swayed them all to bring things to this pass.
Made strong by love, I skilfully deployed
The power I'd been given over him.
The sultans' throne is now within his reach:
Just one step more – but there I wait for him.
If, despite all my love, before tonight
He fails to sign our bond with marriage vows;
If he dares plead the force of hateful law,
And fails to match my courage with his own;
Then instantly, regardless of my love,
And careless whether I destroy myself,
I throw the ingrate off and cast him back
Into the hell from which I drew him forth.
These are the things on which I'll know his mind:
His life or death depends on his reply.
I will not want your services today
Or need your voice to spell my feelings out:
I want myself to see his lips and eyes
Reveal his heart and leave me in no doubt;

I want him led in secret to this place
And brought into my presence unprepared.
Adieu. I'll tell you later all he says.

## ACT ONE, SCENE FOUR: *Atalide, Zaire*

ATALIDE
    Zaire, it's happened – Atalide is lost!

ZAIRE
    Lost?

ATALIDE
        I have seen all I need to see.
    My only hope lies in my loss of hope.

ZAIRE
    But madam, why?

ATALIDE
                You'd know if you had heard
    The deadly course Roxane is set upon,
    The terms that she imposes: Bajazet,
    She says, must die if he'll not marry her.
    What will become of me if he accepts?
    If he refuses, what becomes of him?

ZAIRE
    I understand your plight, but can't believe
    Your love had not anticipated this.

ATALIDE
    O can love be so provident, Zaire?
    It seemed we felt as one on everything;

13

Roxane put all her trust in me, relied
On me to win the heart of Bajazet:
Gave me the care of all that touched on him,
Saw him through my eyes, spoke through my own lips;
I thought the happy moment had arrived
When I, through her, would give my love the crown.
But heaven has shown itself against my plan.
What else was there that I could do, Zaire?
Should I have told Roxane she was mistaken
And lost my love in disabusing her?
Before this love took shape in Roxane's heart
I loved him, and was sure that he loved me.
You will recall that from our earliest years
Our love had sealed the knots which blood had tied.
Reared at his mother's breast with Bajazet
I learnt how little he was like his brother.
She joined our hearts together joyfully
And though we separated at her death,
And never met, we kept the will to please,
And still could love, and still not speak of it.
Roxane, who, unsuspecting, was to seek
My help in furthering her secret plans,
Loved this heart-conquering hero on sight,
And ran to offer her protecting hand.
Bajazet, surprised, was grateful to her,
Paid court to her – and how could he do less?
And yet how quickly love believes its whims!
Convinced by this mere courtesy, Roxane
By her persuasive means engaged us both
To keep her happy in her misbelief.
I must admit my weakness, though, Zaire:
My jealous feelings could not be suppressed:
My rival overwhelmed my love with gifts
And promised empires where I offered none:
Her constant efforts kept her in his thoughts;

She told him of his glory soon to come
Whilst I was powerless. The only words
My heart could speak were sighs, and then more sighs.
Heaven alone saw how much I wept then.
But Bajazet at last dispelled my griefs;
I cursed my tears, and to this day have urged
Dissimulation, whilst I spoke for him.
Alas, it's finished; and the scorned Roxane
Must shortly learn how she's deceived herself.
For Bajazet at last will shun pretence –
I know his courage, quick to save his pride,
And, as his anxious keeper, learnt the need
To make his words sound favourable to her.
He will be lost. If only, as before,
Roxane had used my voice to speak with him!
If only I had warned him how to look!
Zaire, I still can meet him on his way
And save him with a word or with a glance!
He must accept her rather than be killed.
If Roxane wants him dead, there's no escape.
He's lost, I tell you. But wait, Atalide:
Trust in your lover's trust, without alarm.
Do you think you are worth such loss of life?
Perhaps the prince, to make your envy worse,
Will feel more need of life than you would like.

ZAIRE
Madam, why hurl yourself into these cares?
Why take afflictions on before their time?
You cannot doubt you're loved by Bajazet.
Hold off or hide these pains that eat you up:
At all costs don't let tears reveal your loves.
The hand that saved him once will keep him safe
So long as Roxane stays in ignorance
Of her predestined error, and her rival.

Now come away to master your regrets
And wait to learn the outcome of their talk.

ATALIDE
Very good, we'll go. And if your justice, heaven,
Must punish the deceit of two young lovers,
If you condemn our love, O heaven, I
Am more to blame – exhaust your wrath on me.

## ACT TWO, SCENE ONE: *Bajazet, Roxane*

ROXANE

Prince, the fateful hour has come at last
Which heaven has reserved for your release.
Nothing restrains me now, and from this day
I can fulfil the plan my love has laid.
Of course, I do not promise easy triumphs
Or place unchallenged power in your hands;
I do my best, as I am bound to do:
I bolster you against your enemies
And rid your days of a most pressing threat;
The rest, sir, your own courage must accomplish.
Osmin confirms the allegiance of the troops;
The elders of our law conspire with us;
The city is assured by Acomat;
And I have in my power, as you know,
That crowd of ministers and slaves and mutes,
That race confined within the palace walls,
The broken-spirited who long since bought
My favour with their silence and their lives.
Begin at once, ride out into the field
Of glory that I've opened up to you.
You are not entering an unjust course:
Your aim is to repel a murdering hand.
It has been common practice, and a path
To power that the sultans often take.

But for a more auspicious start, let's run
To seal at once your happiness and mine:
Take me to you, and show the universe
That, serving you, I served my own betrothed;
And by the sacred bonds of blessed marriage
Redeem the faith that I have placed in you.

BAJAZET
What are you saying, madam?

ROXANE

                   Now, my lord!
What hidden problem clouds our happiness?

BAJAZET
How can you so forget the empire's pride?
It pains me that you make me speak of this.

ROXANE
O I know that since the time of Bajazet
Who bore the ravages of Tamburlaine
And saw his queen behind the chariot
Dragged chained through Asia by their conqueror,
The sultans have been jealous of their honour
And rarely deigned to take themselves a wife.
But love cannot obey these fancied laws;
I need not give you vulgar instances:
You know that Suleiman – of your forebears,
Who filled the world with fear of their success,
The one who most advanced the Ottomans –
This Suleiman set eyes on Roxelane.
Despite his proud magnificence, this king
Chose her to share his power and his bed –
She who had no claims to be sultaness
Beyond slight charms perhaps and much deceit.

BAJAZET
>  That's true – but then consider my position,
>  What Suleiman then was, what I am now.
>  The power he enjoyed was absolute:
>  He brought back Egypt under his control;
>  Rhodes, that reef the Ottomans so feared,
>  He made the grave of its own garrison;
>  He put the humbled Danube-lands to waste
>  And drove the Persian empire's frontiers back;
>  Whilst in their burning climes the Africans
>  Abandoned their old laws to serve his will.
>  But I – I'm subject to the crowd, the troops;
>  I'm famous only for my miseries.
>  Luckless, banished, doubtful of the throne,
>  Must I enrage the hearts I need to win?
>  Seeing our pleasure, would they share our grief,
>  Or think my dangers and your tears were real?
>  Don't flatter me with talk of Suleiman;
>  Remember how my first poor brother died:
>  In their revolt, the leading janissaries,
>  Who sought a pretext for their blood-soaked scheme,
>  Declared his murder amply justified
>  By such a bond as you propose to me.
>  What can I say to you? Perhaps in time
>  With their support I'll dare to venture more.
>  Let's not be rash; but meanwhile, pray begin
>  To give me power to requite your pains.

ROXANE
>  I understand. I see I have been hasty;
>  That there is nothing you have not foreseen:
>  You have conceived of every slightest harm
>  That my too pressing love could bring upon you.
>  You fear the consequences for your name:
>  And I believe you, since you say it's so.

But have you thought, if you refuse my hand,
Of the more certain dangers that await you?
That without me the world will be against you?
That above all it's me whom you must please?
That I'm the one who holds the palace gates,
Which I can yield or close to you for ever?
That I have total power over you?
That only my love suffers you to breathe?
And that without this love you spurn and pain
You would no longer – in a word – exist?

BAJAZET

I owe you everything; and I believed
That when you saw the empire kneel to me
And heard me swear I owed you everything
You would think that a glory great enough.
I don't deny my debt: I own to it,
And my respect will always make it known:
I owe my life to you; it's yours to use.
But do you want . . .

ROXANE

                No, I want nothing more.
Don't pester me with your forced arguments:
I see how far your heart is from my wishes,
And will not press you, wretch, to yield to them:
Get back into the void I plucked you from.
For what prevents me? And what further proof
Of his indifference could I demand?
Does my quick fervour move the ungrateful wretch?
Are his excuses even touched by love?
I see your plan: no matter what I do
You think the risks I run protect your life;
You think the ties that bind us are too strong
For me to separate our interests.

But my strength is the favour of your brother:
You know he loves me, and for all his rage
I can make full atonement with your blood:
Your death will be enough to pardon me.
Don't doubt me; I will set about it now.
Mark this: I feel I love you, Bajazet:
You damn yourself. Take care to keep me here:
You still have time in which to make amends.
Don't drive me, crazed with passion, to despair:
If I but say the word, your life is gone.

BAJAZET

Take it from me, it is in your hands:
Perhaps my death, in furthering your plans,
And winning thanks from grateful Amurat,
Will give you back your high place in his heart.

ROXANE

His heart? Though he desires that, do you think
That if I lose the hope of ruling yours,
Possessed by that sweet error for so long,
I could endure the thought of other loves,
Or that I even live if not for you?
I arm your cruelty against myself,
No doubt of it; I should retain my weakness,
You'll triumph by it. O yes, I confess,
I put on a false pride to challenge you:
My happiness, my bliss, depend on you –
Your bloody death is followed by my own.
What fruit of all my efforts for your life!
At last you sigh, your features show distress.
Speak, finish it.

BAJAZET

O heavens, how can I speak?

ROXANE

What are you saying? What have I just heard?
You have some secret that I may not share?
What? You have feelings that I may not know?

BAJAZET

Madam, once more it is for you to choose:
Clear me a lawful pathway to the throne;
Or else – I'm ready, strike your victim down.

ROXANE

You go too far – you'll have what you demand.
Guards! Come here!

## ACT TWO, SCENE TWO: *Roxane, Acomat, Bajazet*

ROXANE

Acomat, it's decided.
You can return, there's nothing to be said.
I recognise the rule of Amurat:
Go: henceforth the harem shall be closed,
And all return to its accustomed state.

## ACT TWO, SCENE THREE: *Bajazet, Acomat*

ACOMAT

What have I heard, sir? This is bitter news!
What will become of you? And what of me?
What's brought this change about? Who shall I blame?
O heavens!

BAJAZET
      You must be under no delusions.
Roxane's offended, and she seeks revenge:
A changeless obstacle prevents our plan.
Look to yourself, vizier, I warn you now;
Make your decision – do not count on me.

ACOMAT
  My lord?

BAJAZET
      You and your men must go to ground.
I know how dangerous a friend I am,
And hoped one day to recompense your love.
It's done, I say; better not think of it.

ACOMAT
  But sir, what is this changeless obstacle?
I left the harem in a state of calm:
What madness has possessed your mind and hers?

BAJAZET
  She wants me, Acomat, to marry her.

ACOMAT
  And so? She runs against the custom here,
But does that custom have the force of law
That you must lose your life observing it?
The holiest law says you must save yourself
To keep the ancient line you represent
From the extinction which now threatens it.

BAJAZET
  A bleak survival, and too dearly bought
If it must be maintained by cowardice.

ACOMAT

> Why paint the future in such sombre tones?
> Does marriage dim the fame of Suleiman?
> And bear in mind that he was married free
> Of pressing dangers such as weigh on you.

BAJAZET

> And just such dangers and such self-concern
> Would make this slavish marriage a disgrace.
> Suleiman did not need this vile excuse;
> His slave found favour in his eyes, and he
> Was under no constraint to take his vows.
> His heart was offered to her willingly.

ACOMAT

> But you love Roxane.

BAJAZET

> Acomat, enough.
> My fate dismays me less than you imagine,
> And death is not the worst disgrace to me.
> I braved it as a boy, in your command,
> And in the shameful prison where I'm kept
> Have grown accustomed to it face to face.
> The sultan's shown it me a score of times.
> The life it ends has been a troubled one,
> And if, alas, I leave it with regret . . .
> Forgive me, Acomat, I'm filled with pity
> For all those hearts whose love I can't repay
> Who took me as the object of their hopes.

ACOMAT

> If we die, sir, blame no one but yourself:
> A single word from you can save us all.
> Those janissaries remaining in the town,

The holy guardians of our religion,
Whom the Byzantine people most respect
And hold as the sole shapers of their will,
Are here to lead you to the sacred gate
Where the new sultan always first appears.

BAJAZET

If I'm so dear to them, good Acomat,
Then let them come and seize me from Roxane.
If need be, force the doors of the harem
And enter, followed by your fearless guard.
I'd rather leave here bleeding, scored with blows,
Than burdened with a name I never sought,
Her husband. In the turmoil I may find
Through my despair a way to save myself
And till your cause is certain of success
Fight on, and give you time to come to me.

ACOMAT

But how, for all my efforts, could I keep
Roxane from taking vengeance at a stroke?
And then, what would this exploit have achieved
But to convict your friends of pointless crimes?
Promise that when you're free you will consider
Whether your oath to her holds good or not.

BAJAZET

I!

ACOMAT

Don't blush: you know the Ottomans
Can never slavishly observe their vows.
Think of those heroes whom the right of war
Led to the world's end in victory:
Free in their triumph, masters of their fate,

Their own law the interest of the state.
The throne is holy, but owes half its power
To sworn allegiance that is rarely kept.
I'm losing patience, sir.

BAJAZET

                I know what lengths
They went to in the interest of the state.
But these same kings, though careless of their lives,
Did not redeem themselves by perfidy.

ACOMAT

O changeless courage! O too constant faith,
That even as I perish I admire!
And must one moment's timid scruple lose . . .
But what good fortune brings us Atalide?

ACT TWO, SCENE FOUR: *Bajazet, Atalide, Acomat*

ACOMAT

O madam, join your voice to mine, he's lost.

ATALIDE

That's what I've come to speak to him about.
But leave us; Roxane, quickened by his loss,
Has ordered that the palace gates be barred.
Whatever happens, Acomat, stay close,
For you may soon be needed here again.

ACT TWO, SCENE FIVE: *Bajazet, Atalide*

BAJAZET

Ah well! the time has come when we must part.
Heaven damns my pretence and scorns your skill;

Nothing has armed me for these latest blows:
Either I die or I surrender you.
What good has our unworthy caution done us?
I die a little later, that is all.
It is as I foresaw, but as you wished:
I saved you from your grieving while I could.
Fair Atalide, for that sweet duty's sake
I beg you, shun the presence of Roxane:
Your weeping would betray you, hide it from her;
And put an end to dangerous farewells.

ATALIDE

No, sir. Your goodness to a hapless soul
Has fought against your destiny too long.
The cost to you of sparing me's too great.
I yield; you must leave me and take the throne.

BAJAZET

Leave you?

ATALIDE

         I wish it. I have searched my heart.
It's true that eaten up with jealous cares
I could not till this moment contemplate
A world in which you lived and were not mine;
And when sometimes I pictured to myself
My lucky rival in a state of grief
Your death (forgive the wildness of a lover)
Seemed not the worst of agonies to me.
But my sad eyes had not imagined then
The death that will be yours in all its horror.
I did not see you, as I see you now,
Prepared to say farewell for the last time.
My lord, I know too well the constancy
With which you will confront the face of death;

27

I know the pleasure that your heart will find
In proving its own honour as it dies.
But spare a spirit far less resolute;
Match your misfortunes to my strength to bear them;
Don't leave your Atalide the prey to griefs
Keener than ever drew a lover's tears.

BAJAZET

But what becomes of you if in your sight
I go to take these fatal marriage-vows?

ATALIDE

Don't ask to know what will become of me.
I may submit, sir, to my destiny.
Who knows? I'll seek an antidote to grief.
Perhaps in weeping I'll recall how you
Had been prepared to lose your life for me,
And that you live because I wished you to.

BAJAZET

No, this cruel marriage never shall take place.
The more you urge me to be false to you,
Madam, the more I see how you deserve
Never to obtain what you desire.
This tender love, born when you were a child,
Whose fires have grown in silence as we grew;
Your tears that only I had power to stop;
My frequent vows that I will never leave you:
Can all these things die by my treachery?
I'd marry – but whom, if the truth be told?
A slave, moved only by her own concerns,
Who tortures me with visions of my end,
Who offers me her hand or else my death;
Whilst Atalide, who feels for my distress
And is too worthy of her noble blood,

Prepares to sacrifice herself for me?
If that's the price at which it must be bought
Then let the jealous sultan have my head.

ATALIDE

Sir, you can live, and still be true to me.

BAJAZET

Speak; I will obey you if I can.

ATALIDE

The sultaness loves you; despite her anger,
If you could take more care to flatter her,
And if your sighs could lead her to believe
One day . . .

BAJAZET

        I understand, but can't consent.
You mustn't think, as this long day wears on,
That my resolve is weakened by despair,
Or that I fear the throne that could be mine
And seek to be excused its cares in death.
I am too moved perhaps by reckless daring;
My mighty forebears ever fill my mind,
Exhorting me to flee my idleness
And take my place in their heroic line.
But still, whatever thirst for love or power
Burns me, I cannot betray your trust.
I would have sworn to save myself in vain:
My eyes and lips, repelled by all untruth,
Would surely, when I sought to bring her joy,
Have in their turmoil told another story.
Whilst she, offended by my frigid sighs,
Would know that they did not express my heart.
Heavens! how often I'd have told the truth

29

If I alone was threatened by her hate
And if I had not feared her jealousy
Would all too readily rebound on you!
And I should trick her with a false avowal,
Perjure myself, and by such base designs . . ?
Ah, if your heart were less full of its love
I know that I would see you blush the first
At calling for so shameful an evasion.
But I will spare you your unjust entreaty:
Farewell – I go at once to find Roxane,
And so I leave you.

ATALIDE

                I will not leave you.
Come, cruel man, come – I'll take you to her.
I want to be the one to tell our secrets:
Since, despite my tears, my raging lover
Takes such delight in dying in my sight,
Roxane, in spite of him, shall join our fates:
She'll be more thirsty for my blood than yours;
She'll let me stage before your sickened eyes
The spectacle that you rehearse for me.

BAJAZET

O heavens, what are you doing?

ATALIDE

                    Can you think
I am less jealous of my name than you?
That on the hundred times I spoke for you
My blushes did not threaten to expose me?
But I was faced with your impending death.
Why then, ungrateful wretch, when mine is sure,
Do you not dare for me as I for you?
Perhaps a gentler word is what's required;

Perhaps Roxane forgives you in her heart.
You see yourself the time she has let pass.
Did she send out the vizier when you parted?
Have guards been sent to take you from my sight?
And when, in her distress, she craved my help,
Did not her tears show me her tenderness?
Perhaps she only needs a sign of hope
Before she drops the weapon from her hand.
Go, my lord, and save your life and mine.

BAJAZET

But what is it you'd have me say to her?

ATALIDE

O don't consult me on your choice of words!
Those heaven and the occasion will dictate.
Go – I cannot be with you and her,
Our agitation would betray our hearts.
Go – again, I dare not come with you.
Say . . . what you must, my lord, to save yourself.

## ACT THREE, SCENE ONE: *Atalide, Zaire*

ATALIDE

    Zaire, so is it true, and he is pardoned?

ZAIRE

    I've told you, madam: a swift-footed slave
    Who ran to carry out Roxane's desire
    Has met the vizier at the harem gates.
    They did not speak to me, but more than words
    The rapture of the vizier's face confirmed
    It was some happy change that brought him here
    And that he comes to sign eternal peace.
    It's clear Roxane has chosen gentler ways.

ATALIDE

    So on all sides my pleasures and my joy
    Abandon me, Zaire, and take their leave.
    I've done all that I could; I've no regrets.

ZAIRE

    Now, madam, what new consternation's this?

ATALIDE

    Did no one tell you, Zaire, by what charm,
    Or what commitments, to be more exact,
    The prince has brought about this sudden change?

Roxane appeared inflexible with rage:
Has she secured true tokens of his love?
Speak. Will he marry her?

ZAIRE

                    I do not know.
But if his life could not be bought for less;
If he has done as you yourself advised
And married her . . .

ATALIDE

             And married her, Zaire!

ZAIRE

Do you regret the generous words you spoke
When your concern was all to save his life?

ATALIDE

No, no: he'll do no more than is required.
If Bajazet weds her, he does my will.
O jealous feelings, keep your silence now:
Respect my courage in surmounting you;
Don't cloud my noble counsel with your own;
Rather than thinking of him in her arms
Let me imagine him without regrets
Upon the throne I forced him to accept.
O yes, I know myself, I'm still the same.
I wanted him to love me and he does.
I find some consolation in my hope
Of dying worthily and proud of him.

ZAIRE

Of dying! Can you have so grim a plan?

ATALIDE

    I've given up my love – are you surprised?
    Can you consider my death a misfortune
    If it will save and solve so many griefs?
    It is enough he lives. It's as I wished;
    And I still wish it, though it costs me dear.
    I give no thought to my own joy or pain:
    I love my love enough to give him up –
    Though he alas may think, and with good cause,
    If I can make this sacrifice for him,
    My heart, that bears these dread cares for his life,
    Loves him too much to live and see it done.
    Come, I need to know . . .

ZAIRE

                For pity's sake
    Be calm, and you will learn what they have said.

## ACT THREE, SCENE TWO: *Atalide, Acomat, Zaire*

ACOMAT

    Madam, our lovers have agreed at last;
    A happy calm returns us to the port.
    Roxane has let her anger be disarmed:
    She has announced to me her firm intent:
    Whilst she unfurls the holy prophet's flag
    Before the awestruck people, and the prince
    Prepares himself to follow where I lead,
    I am to make the signal's meaning known,
    Fill every spirit with a righteous fear,
    And then proclaim the new-crowned emperor.
    Meanwhile permit me to recall to you
    The prize that I was promised for my zeal.
    Do not expect such sweet transports from me

As I have witnessed in these lovers' hearts;
But if, by cares more suited to my age,
By deep respect and the long slavery
We owe to those who share our sultan's blood
I can . . .

ATALIDE

You can inform me in due course.
In due course, too, you'll have the chance to know me.
But what are these transports they let you see?

ACOMAT

Madam, you cannot doubt the burning sighs
Of two young lovers so lost in each other?

ATALIDE

No; though I confess I am astonished.
And is the price of Roxane's pardon known?
Is he to marry her?

ACOMAT

I think he is.
I'll tell you everything I have just seen.
Shocked at their mutual rage, I must confess,
And sick of lovers, love and destiny,
I'd left the palace precincts in despair,
And on a vessel ready in the port,
Loading dear relics saved from my disgrace,
I pondered an escape to foreign lands.
Called to the palace from these sorry plans,
Filled with new joy and hope I ran, I flew.
The harem doors were opened at my voice
And there a slave-girl was awaiting me
Who led me noiselessly into a room
Where Roxane listened closely to her lover.

All kept a solemn silence in their presence:
And I myself, controlling my impatience,
Respectful of their secret colloquy,
Unmoving, watched them long and from afar.
And in the end, with eyes that bared her soul,
She gave her hand as token of her passion;
And he, with speaking looks of love, in turn
Gave his assurance, madam, of his heart.

ATALIDE

Alas!

ACOMAT

And then in turn they saw me there.
'You see,' she said to me, 'your prince and mine.
Good Acomat, I leave him in your hands.
Go and prepare the sovereign rites for him;
Gather our subject people in the temple:
The harem will be first, and show the way.'
I threw myself before the prince's feet,
And then at once I vanished from their sight,
Delighted that in passing I could give
A true account of their accord to you
And so confirm to you my deep respect.
I go to crown him, madam, rest assured.

## ACT THREE, SCENE THREE: *Atalide, Zaire*

ATALIDE

Let us withdraw, let's not disturb their joy.

ZAIRE

Ah, madam! do you think . . .

ATALIDE

                      What can I think?
Well, what? Can I be witness to this scene?
You see it is decided, they will marry;
He swears he loves Roxane, and she's content.
Yet I have no complaint, it's as I wished.
But did you ever think, when proudly true
He went to sacrifice himself for me;
When, pouring out his tenderness to me
He then denied Roxane a simple word;
When all my tears had tried in vain to move him
And I found glory in their lack of power,
Did you think that his heart, against such odds,
Would find the eloquence to bring her round?
Perhaps it was quite easy after all,
And everything that he could say, he felt.
Perhaps, on seeing her, he liked her more
And found some new enchantment in her eyes;
She will have spoken of her griefs to him;
She loves him; there's an empire in her tears:
Such love will touch a generous heart at last.
Alas, what arguments for my despair!

ZAIRE

But madam, such an outcome's still unsure.
Be patient.

ATALIDE

             No, denying it is vain,
I take no joy in adding to my pain;
I knew what he must do to save himself.
When my tears drew him back towards Roxane
I never claimed he did not do my will.
But after the farewells I had just heard
And all the transports of his tender grief

I know that he should not have shown the joy
And rapture I'm now told that he showed her.
You be our judge, and see if I am wrong:
Why was I not consulted in this plan?
Is my part in his destiny so slight?
Would he delay so long to seek me out
Did not the just reproach of his own heart
Cause him, alas, to hesitate and stay?
But no, I'd like to spare him that distress:
He'll not see me again.

ZAIRE

                Madam, he's here.

## ACT THREE, SCENE FOUR: *Bajazet, Atalide, Zaire*

BAJAZET
It's done, I've spoken, you have been obeyed.
You need have no more fears for my life;
And I would be content if trust and honour
Did not begrudge me my unjust good fortune;
And if my heart, vexed, speechless and condemned,
Could pardon me as lightly as Roxane.
But I have weapons in my hands at last;
I'm free; and can oppose my cruel brother –
Not silently, and aided by your skill,
Disputing his own mistress's affections,
But in real combat and through noble dangers,
Seeking him out myself in foreign lands,
Disputing the affections of our army
And letting good renown stand judge between us.
But what is this? You're weeping?

ATALIDE
                              No, my lord,
I'll breathe no word against your happiness.
It is a miracle the heavens owed you,
And one you know I never tried to hinder:
You are my witness that, while I still lived,
My thoughts were filled with nothing but your plight;
And since your plight continues till I die
I sacrifice myself without regrets.
It's true, if heaven had listened to my vows
It could have granted me a happier death:
You could have wed my rival just the same,
You could have promised her a husband's trust,
But you would not have marked your married state
With all the show of love she's had from you.
She would have thought herself well recompensed:
And I could die secure in the sweet thought
That having made this law for you myself
I sent you to her full of love for me,
That I took all your passion to the grave
And did not leave you to her as a lover.

BAJAZET
What is this talk of husbands and of lovers,
Madam? Heavens, what's behind these words?
Who can have given you this false account?
I, madam, love Roxane, or live for her?
Can you believe that I could think such things,
Much less that I could put them into words?
No, neither thoughts nor words were necessary:
The sultaness pursued her normal course,
And whether she at first saw my return
As a sure sign that I returned her love
Or whether precious time forced her to yield,
I'd barely spoken what she barely heard

Before her sudden weeping silenced me:
She put her life and fortune in my hands,
And, trusting in my gratitude, expressed
Her hope that we would marry without fail.
I blushed to see how she deceived herself,
How little I deserved her tender love,
And in my discomposure, which Roxane
Attributed to a passionate excess,
I found myself wild, unjust, criminal.
Believe me, in that cruel interval
I kept my lying silence to the end
Only by calling up my love for you.
But still, when after such a task, I come
To seek some respite for my own remorse
I find you turned against me in disdain,
Blaming your death on my unquiet soul.
I see at last, I see that even now
You're scarcely touched by what I say to you.
Madam, let's end your misery and mine,
Let's end our vain affliction of each other.
Roxane's close by; let my good faith be seen:
I'll go, far more content with both of us,
To disabuse her of this forced pretence,
Than when I went just now and hid my thoughts.
She's here.

ATALIDE

       Great heavens! what will he disclose?
You'll tell her nothing if you care for me.

ACT THREE, SCENE FIVE: *Bajazet, Roxane, Atalide*

ROXANE

Come, my lord, come: it's time you should appear,
And the harem pay tribute to its master:
All the crowd of people that it shelters,
Gathered at my command, await my will.
The slaves I own, whom all the rest will follow,
Are the first subjects my love offers you.
Would you have thought it, madam, that such hate
Could yield so swiftly to so great a love?
A moment back, set wholly on revenge,
I swore that he was living his last day:
And yet when he had barely said a word
Love broke the oath which love itself had made.
Through his confusion I had glimpsed his heart:
I spoke his pardon, and accept his word.

BAJAZET

Yes, I have promised you upon my word
I will remember all I owe to you;
I've sworn that in my just desire to please
My cares shall always demonstrate my debt.
If I deserve your kindness on those terms
I wait to see the fruits of your goodwill.

ACT THREE, SCENE SIX: *Roxane, Atalide*

ROXANE

I am dumbfounded with astonishment!
Can I be dreaming? Have my eyes deceived me?
What is this sombre welcome, these iced words
That seem to undo all that went before?
What hope of mine does he think made me yield

And give him back the friendship he had lost?
I thought he swore to me that, unto death,
His love would leave me mistress of his fate.
Can he so soon repent the peace we made?
Or can I have deceived myself just now?
Ah! but he spoke to you: what was he saying,
Madam?

ATALIDE

      I, madam! That he loves you still.

ROXANE

His life, and not his life alone, depends
On my believing that; yet how, when he
Has so much cause for joy, can you explain
The vexed disdain he showed me as he left?

ATALIDE

Madam, I was aware of no disdain.
He spoke to me at length of your kind deeds,
And when I met him was quite full of them.
I felt he left here much as he had come.
Is it surprising, madam, after all,
If, poised to carry off this great affair,
Bajazet is anxious, or lets slip
Some sign of all the cares that fill his mind?

ROXANE

You are too artful in excusing him:
You do it better than he can himself.

ATALIDE

What other interest . . .

ROXANE
                    Madam, enough:
I know your reasons better than you think.
Leave me: I need a moment's solitude.
I too am rendered anxious by this day:
Like Bajazet, I have my rankling cares,
And wish to ponder them unheard a while.


## ACT THREE, SCENE SEVEN: *Roxane*

ROXANE
What can I think of all that I have seen?
Are they in league to keep the truth from me?
Why change, and speak, and go away like that?
Indeed, did I not see them share a glance?
Bajazet desperate! Atalide dismayed!
O heaven, would you condemn me to such shame?
Can these be all the fruits of my blind love?
So many sorry days and restless nights;
My intrigues, plots, and fateful treachery –
Can I have risked all this to help a rival?
It may be I distress myself too soon
And misconstrue a passing discontent,
Faulting his love for what is mere caprice.
Would he not play his trick out to the end?
With his deceit in sight of victory,
What! would he not pretend a moment more?
No, rest assured: it's love that makes me quail.
And why fear Atalide's place in his heart?
What could her plan be? How has she served him?
Which of us, after all, crowns him today?
And yet, do we know nothing of love's power?
If Atalide lures him with other charms
What matter that he owes me life and crown?

43

Are benefits love's equal in a heart?
And when his brother wooed me, can I say
I gave him warmer thanks than he gives me?
O if he were not bound by other chains
Would my proposal so have frightened him?
Would he not gladly have obeyed my will?
Would he have risked his life to turn me down?
How many worthy reasons . . . But who's here?
What do you want?

## ACT THREE, SCENE EIGHT: *Roxane, Zatime*

ZATIME

                Forgive my troubling you;
A slave has reached us, madam, from the army,
And though he found the sea-gates closed, the guards
At once, on bended knee, admitted him
At Amurat's command, addressed to you.
Yet what dismays me – he has sent Orcan.

ROXANE

Orcan!

ZATIME

           Yes, of all whom he employs,
Orcan, whom he most trusts to do his will,
Born in the fires of blackest Africa.
Madam, he asks for you impatiently.
But I knew I must warn you in advance;
And anxious lest he take you by surprise
Have brought him to your quarters, where he waits.

ROXANE

What further unguessed torment comes to blast me?
What can this order be, or my response?
The troubled sultan, there can be no doubt,
Condemns his brother for a second time.
No one can take his life unless I say:
Here all obey me. Should I save him, though?
Is Bajazet my king or Amurat?
One may be false, the other I've betrayed.
Time presses. How to end this dreadful doubt?
We'll go, and use the moment left to us.
They cannot hide themselves – the tightest love
Lets slip its secret in some little sign.
We'll watch the prince, but her we'll terrify:
Then crown him if he's true – if not, destroy.

## ACT FOUR, SCENE ONE: *Atalide, Zaire*

ATALIDE

Ah, can you guess my fright? I have just seen
Wild Orcan's hateful face in the harem.
O, how I fear his coming at this time!
But tell me, did you speak to Bajazet?
What did he say? Will he do as I asked?
Will he seek out Roxane and calm her doubts?

ZAIRE

He cannot see her unless she commands:
Which she has done, she bids him to attend.
No doubt she wants to hide him from this slave.
I sought him out, pretending I did not,
Gave him your letter, and took his reply.
You shall see, madam, what it has to say.

ATALIDE (*reads*)

        'After so many cruel delays
Why must your love still urge me to pretend?
        But I want to protect the life
          On which you swear your own depends.
I'll see the sultaness, be kind to her,
And by new oaths of my indebtedness
        Appease her fury if I can.
Ask nothing more: not death, not you yourself

Will ever make me tell her I love her:
> For I love none but you alone.'

Alas! does he think he need tell me that?
Do I not know he loves me, dotes on me?
Is this how he accedes to my request?
It is Roxane he must persuade, not me.
What is this fear that he still leaves me with?
Zaire, if possible, go back to him:
*Appeasing* her is not enough for me.
His lips, his eyes, must prove his love to her:
Let her at last believe it. Couldn't I
Speak for him, warm his efforts with my tears,
Transforming them with what I feel for him?
I fear new dangers I'd expose him to.

## ACT FOUR, SCENE TWO: *Roxane, Atalide, Zatime, Zaire*

ROXANE (*to Zatime*)
I have the order. Now we'll frighten her.

ATALIDE (*to Zaire*)
Go, run; try to prevail on him at last.

## ACT FOUR, SCENE THREE: *Roxane, Atalide, Zatime*

ROXANE
Madam, I have letters from the siege.
Are you aware of all that's happened there?

ATALIDE
I heard a slave had reached us from the camp:
Beyond that all is unknown to me still.

47

ROXANE

The sultan is content: his fortune's changed,
And Babylon pays homage to his rule.

ATALIDE

But madam, how? Osmin . . .

ROXANE

Was ill informed;
The slave we have received left after him.
The sultan follows close behind himself.

ATALIDE

What? the armed Persians do not hold him back?

ROXANE

No, madam: he rejoins us with all speed.

ATALIDE

Madam, I pity you; you must be quick
To finish off what you have planned to do.

ROXANE

It's late to turn against the conqueror.

ATALIDE

O heavens!

ROXANE

Time has not softened his harsh ways.
I have his supreme ordinance in my hands.

ATALIDE

What does he say?

ROXANE

        See – read it for yourself.
You know the writing and the signature.

ATALIDE

    I know the hand of cruel Amurat.
    (*reads*) 'Before my might had shaken Babylon
    I sent my absolute commands to you.
    I do not want to think I'm disobeyed,
    And trust that Bajazet no longer lives.
    I have brought Babylon beneath my sway,
    And as I leave confirm my royal decree.
    You, if you have regard for your own life,
    Will welcome me with his head in your hands.'

ROXANE
    Well?

ATALIDE (*aside*)
    Hide your tears, unhappy Atalide.

ROXANE
    What do you think?

ATALIDE

        He holds his murderous course –
    But thinks the prince he kills has no support:
    He does not know the love he feels for you;
    That you and Bajazet are of one soul;
    That if need be you'd rather die . . .

ROXANE

                I, madam?
    I'd like to save a man I cannot hate;
    But . . .

ATALIDE
What have you decided?

ROXANE
                      To obey.

ATALIDE
Obey!

ROXANE
     What else? The danger is so great:
I must.

ATALIDE
      You mean this sweet prince . . . who loves you . . .
Must see the life he's given to you end!

ROXANE
He must; I have already ordered it.

ATALIDE
I die.

ZATIME
     She falls – she barely clings to life.

ROXANE
Go, lead her into the next room, Zatime;
Be sure to note her looks, and what she says –
Anything that proves their treacherous love.

## ACT FOUR, SCENE FOUR: *Roxane*

ROXANE
My rival's shown herself to me at last.
Such is the honour I relied upon!
For six whole months I've thought that night and day
She watched over my love devotedly:
And it is I, more faithful than I knew,
Who for six months have ministered to her;
Who've set myself the task of finding ways
To bring about their happy interviews;
And who, anticipating his desires,
Hastened the sweetest moments of his life.
That is not all: I must discover now
If she succeeded in her treachery;
I must . . . But what more do I need to know?
My own misfortune's written in her face.
Can I not see, beyond her faint, a heart
That suffers but is happy in its love?
Free from all the doubts that torture me,
She fears, but only for her lover's life.
No matter: I must find out. She, like me,
May base her trust on pledges falsely given.
To make him show himself, let's set a trap.
But would I set myself so low a task?
What? take the trouble to exert my wits
Only to have his scorn burst in my face?
He might foresee my trick – trick me himself.
Besides, slave, edict, vizier press on me:
I must decide – they wait. A better plan:
Let's close our eyes to all that we have seen;
Forget the tiresome probing of their love;
Let's push him to the limit, tempt our fate,
And see, when I have raised him to the throne,
If he will dare betray my saving love,

If, indolently free with what I gave,
He'll dare to offer Atalide the crown.
I'll always find occasion, if need be,
To punish both my rival and her love:
In righteous anger, if I find him false,
I can surprise him with his Atalide,
And with a single dagger join their hearts,
Stab both of them, and after them, myself.
That without doubt's the course that I must take.
I must know nothing.

## ACT FOUR, SCENE FIVE: *Roxane, Zatime*

ROXANE

              Ah, what must I hear,
Zatime? Is Bajazet in love with her?
Does what she says convince you of their bond?

ZATIME

She has not spoken, madam: in her swoon
She lies and shows no other sign of life
Than long-drawn sighs and shudders that it seems
Her heart itself must any moment follow.
Your women, caring for her as yourself,
Have bared her breast to let her seizure work.
I helped them to perform this urgent task
And in her bosom found this letter hidden:
I recognised the prince your lover's hand,
And felt that I should bring it straight to you.

ROXANE

Give it me ... Why tremble? What new dread
Chills me to see this thing, makes my hand shake?
It could be done without offence to me;

52

He even might . . . Let's read, and see his thought:
'. . . . . . not death, not you yourself
Will ever make me tell her I love her:
      For I love none but you alone.'
Now I have had a lesson in betrayal!
I see the bait they have seduced me with.
This then is how my love was recompensed,
Coward, unworthy of the life I spared!
I breathe at last, and I am overjoyed
To find the traitor has betrayed himself.
Freed from the pains I was about to take
My calm contempt need only take revenge.
He dies: we are avenged. Run: have him seized;
And let my mutes arm for his execution;
Have them come and dress the fierce garrotte
By which the days of all such men must end.
Run, Zatime, quick servant of my anger!

ZATIME

  O madam!

ROXANE

      What?

ZATIME

         I risk your further wrath
In daring, when I see you justly moved,
To make you hear this timid plea of mine:
It's true that Bajazet's too base to live
And should be put into your murderers' hands;
But even so, do you believe that he
Is more to fear than Amurat today?
Who knows, the sultan may have heard by now
Of your new love from some false-trusted tongue.
Madam, hearts like his, as you well know,
Never regain themselves once they are crossed;

53

At such grim moments, then the swiftest death
Becomes the dearest witness of their love.

ROXANE

But with what insolence and cruelty
The two of them have trifled with my trust!
What rightful joy I felt, believing them!
You did not win a mighty victory,
Betrayer, when you tricked this troubled heart,
Which feared, itself, to be so disabused.
I, who from high rank that made me proud
In depths of misery sought you the first
To banish the dark threats that hedged you round
With promises of blest and tranquil days,
After such care and kindness, utmost pains,
Must learn that you will never say you love me.
What memories are these I stray among?
Sad girl, you're weeping! O, you should have wept
When vain desire first roused you to your fate,
When first you formed the wish to look on him.
You're weeping! whilst the prince, poised to betray,
Prepares the words he hopes will dazzle you;
To please your rival, he preserves his life.
Ah! traitor, you shall die! What, still not gone?
Go. But let us go ourself, make haste:
Attentive to the details of his death
I'll show him both his brother's ordinance
And this firm token of his treachery.
You, hold my rival fast within these walls.
He'll die with her cries as his sole farewell.
Meanwhile let her be loyally waited on;
Take care of her: my hate needs her alive.
Ah, if she melts so easily for him
She almost dies for terror of his death
How much the sweeter will be my revenge

So soon to show him to her, lifeless, pale,
To see her staring eyes, fixed on that thing,
Pay back the pleasures I have let them have.
Go, keep her in. Keep silence above all.
I . . . But who comes to turn revenge aside?

## ACT FOUR, SCENE SIX: *Roxane, Acomat, Osmin*

ACOMAT
What are you doing, madam? Why delay
A single moment of this precious day?
The mass of the townspeople whom I've raised
Question their leaders, troubled by their fear;
And they, and all my friends, for explanation
Await the signal you have promised me.
Why is it that neglectful of their mood
The harem keeps this mournful silence still?
Madam, declare yourself, without delay . . .

ROXANE
Yes, rest content, I will declare myself.

ACOMAT
The sternness of your voice and manner, madam,
Despite your words, convinces me you will not.
What, has your love already bowed to fate . . .

ROXANE
Bajazet is false. He's lived too long.

ACOMAT
False!

ROXANE

     Equally untrue to me and you,
He tricked us both.

ACOMAT

           But how?

ROXANE

                This Atalide,
Who would not even make a worthy prize
For you, and all that you have done for him . . .

ACOMAT
  Well?

ROXANE

     Read: and judge, after such insolence,
Whether the traitor merits our defence.
Rather obey the just severity
Of Amurat, whose triumph is at hand,
Gladly give our base accomplice up,
And seek reprieve in his prompt sacrifice.

ACOMAT (*giving back the letter*)
Since he dares hold me in such deep contempt
I will myself avenge you if need be,
Madam. While he still lives we stand accused
Of crimes his death at once absolves us from.
Show me the way, I'll go.

ROXANE

             No, Acomat:
Leave me the pleasure of confounding him.
I revel in his shame and his dismay.
I'd lose my vengeance if I made it quick.
I shall prepare each detail. You, meanwhile,
Dismiss with all speed your assembled friends.

## ACT FOUR, SCENE SEVEN: *Acomat, Osmin*

ACOMAT

Wait: it's not yet time for me to go.

OSMIN

What! your love brings you to this, my lord?
Have you not taken vengeance far enough?
Would you now be a witness to his death?

ACOMAT

What do you mean? Are you so credulous
As to impute such stupid rage to me?
I jealous? Would to heaven I alone
Had suffered from the prince's foolishness!

OSMIN

But sir, why didn't you defend him then . . .

ACOMAT

And was Roxane in any state to hear me?
Did you not see that when I sought her out
It was with him I lost or saved myself?
Unhappy outcome of so many plans!
Blind prince! – or should I say, blind minister?
It well becomes me, rich in years and state,
To have put all my trust in such young hands,
And let my baseless fortune as vizier
Float in the wake of these rash lovers' acts!

OSMIN

O let them use their anger on each other.
Bajazet seeks death; my lord, think of yourself.
Who could reveal the mystery of your plans
Beyond a few friends sworn to secrecy?
You'll see the sultan softened by his death.

ACOMAT

Roxane beside herself may reason so,
But I, who take a longer view and know
From long experience the thoughts of kings;
Who've aged, from post to post, beneath three reigns
And seen my predecessors' grim rewards,
I know beyond a doubt that men like me
Find favour only through audacity,
And that a bloody death is all the bond
A slave has with the master he offends.

OSMIN

Then flee.

ACOMAT

           I thought the same until just now:
But then my enterprise was less advanced;
Now it's too difficult for turning back.
I must seek glory in a noble fall
And leave at least a ruin when I flee
To hinder the pursuit of enemies.
Bajazet still lives: why be amazed?
Acomat's rescued him from worser fates.
Let's save him from this danger and himself,
For us, our friends, and even for Roxane.
You saw the way her heart protected him
And stayed my sudden offer of revenge.
I'm ignorant of love, but dare be sworn
Although she seeks his downfall he's not lost;
We still have time. In spite of her despair
Roxane still loves him, and will go to him.

OSMIN

What gives you such high courage in the end?
If Roxane orders us, then we must go:
This place is overrun . . .

ACOMAT
With unknown slaves

Bred here within the palace, far from war;
But you, whose valour, which the king forgets,
Binds our two fates through common grievances,
Will you be with me fearless to the end?

OSMIN

My lord, you slight me: if you die, I die.

ACOMAT

A fearsome gathering of troops and friends
Awaits our coming at the palace gates;
The sultaness relies on what I say:
Raised in the harem, I know all its ways;
I know the place where Bajazet is lodged;
No more delay, let's go; if we must die
Let's die: I as a vizier, and you,
Dear Osmin, as a vizier's favourite.

## ACT FIVE, SCENE ONE: *Atalide*

ATALIDE
Alas! I search in vain: it can't be found.
O wretched woman, how can you have lost it?
Heaven, is it your will my fatal love
So often should betray its cause today?
Or that the ill-starred letter should have found
Its way to her so soon – the latest blow?
I stood on this same spot: my fearful hand,
When Roxane entered, hid it in my breast.
Her presence overwhelmed my grieving heart:
Her threats, her voice, an order troubled me:
I felt my strength and spirits ebb away:
When I came to, her women hemmed me round;
Then fled as one from my astonished gaze.
O cruel hands that offered me your help –
Inhuman help, bought at too high a price;
It's you who put this letter in her grasp.
What plans have occupied her thoughts since then?
Who'll be the first on whom her vengeance falls?
What blood can satisfy her jealousy?
O, Bajazet is dead, or dying now,
Whilst I am seized and held a prisoner here.
There's someone coming: I'm to learn his fate.

ACT FIVE, SCENE TWO: *Roxane, Atalide, Zatime*

ROXANE
Withdraw.

ATALIDE
              Madam, forgive my disarray . . .

ROXANE
Withdraw, I say; and do not answer me.
Guards, take her in.

ACT FIVE, SCENE THREE: *Roxane, Zatime*

ROXANE
                    Yes, all's prepared, Zatime;
The mutes await their victim with Orcan.
Yet I am still the mistress of his fate:
I can retain him. If he leaves, he's dead.
He's coming?

ZATIME
              A slave brings him close behind:
And far from guessing his impending death
It seemed to me he left his lodging-place
With hasty eagerness to find you, madam.

ROXANE
O coward soul, deserving his abuse,
Can you still bear to have him come to you?
Or dream your words could conquer or amaze?
If he surrendered, could you pardon him?
What? Should you not already be avenged?
Do you not think you've been reviled enough?

Rather than toil so hard for his cold heart
Why don't you let him die? . . . But here he is.

## ACT FIVE, SCENE FOUR: *Bajazet, Roxane*

ROXANE
   I'll spare you any trivial reproach:
   Time is too precious to be lost in talk.
   You've known my mercy: in a word, you live –
   And what I tell you you already know.
   If, for all my love, I have not pleased you,
   I've no complaint; although to tell the truth
   I hoped that that same love, those same kind deeds,
   Perhaps might have made good my fading charms.
   But in the end I'm staggered that for thanks,
   And as reward for so much love and trust,
   You have so long, and with such sordid tricks,
   Pretended to a love you did not feel.

BAJAZET
   Who, madam, I?

ROXANE
               Yes, you. Don't you still want
   Your scorn of me to flourish undiscerned?
   Do you not hope by false appearances
   To hide the love which claims your heart elsewhere,
   And with a traitor's tongue to swear to me
   What you feel only for your Atalide?

BAJAZET
   Atalide! O heavens, madam, who . . .

ROXANE
Traitor, take, see, can you disown this hand?

BAJAZET
I can say nothing more: this honest letter
Holds all the mystery of a thwarted love;
The secret you now know was ripe for telling:
A thousand times I've longed to make it known.
I love, I do admit it, and before
You guessed my need for love and spoke your own
My heart was taken with this life-long passion
And closed against all other wild desires.
You offered me the empire and my life;
And, if I dare say this to you, your love,
Trusting the power of these gifts, dreamt up
The sentiments of mine you wished to hear.
I knew your error, but what could I do,
Seeing as well how dear it was to you?
How fiercely the throne tempts ambitious souls!
Your gift's magnificence unsealed my eyes
And without more ado I took the chance
I longed for to break free of slavery –
The more so since I must accept or die,
The more so since on fire with zeal to give
You dreaded my refusal most of all,
Since even my rejection would expose you,
And having dared to see and speak to me
You were in danger if you changed your mind.
And even so, your own complaints attest
I hardly tricked you with false promises.
Think how many times you have reproached
My silence – witness to a hidden pain:
As your success and my accession neared
The more my baffled heart reproached itself.
At the same time, as heaven, which heard me, knows,

I was not set on impotent desires:
And if at last the outcome, as I hoped,
Had left me free to show my gratitude,
I would, by so much honour and respect
Have satisfied your pride and paid my debts
That you yourself perhaps . . .

ROXANE

What could you do?
Unless you gave your heart, how could you please me?
What would the dead fruit of your vows have been?
Have you forgotten everything I am?
Mistress of this harem, judge of your life,
And even, since the state is in my trust,
Sultaness, and ruler of a heart
That loves me only, such as yours is not:
In this high eminence I have attained
What worthless honour had you kept me for?
Should I drag out my sad fate in these halls,
Vile cast-off of the wretch whom I had crowned,
Fallen from glory, equal with the crowd,
Or even my own rival's favoured slave?
Forget these idle words: no more deceit:
Say, for the last time, will you live and reign?
I hold your sentence, and can save you from it.
You've but a moment: speak.

BAJAZET

What must I do?

ROXANE

My rival's waiting: come with me at once
To see her death-throes, strangled by my mutes:
Then, freed from passions fatal to your name,
Commit yourself to me: time does the rest.
This is your pardon's price, if you will pay.

BAJAZET

> I only could accept to punish you,
> To make the empire see beyond a doubt
> The loathing that your offer fills me with.
> Yet being swept away with rage like this
> I stir your hatred of her own sad life.
> She bears no part whatever in my rage,
> Nor in my love, nor my ingratitude:
> So far from binding me with jealous counsel
> She would have made me yours had I obeyed.
> Acknowledging your goodness and your charms
> She wept in her attempt to bring me round;
> Prepared for sacrifice, a score of times
> She sought to bind me to you by her death.
> Pray, separate her virtue from my crime.
> Pursue your lawful anger if you must:
> Be swift to carry out the sultan's will;
> But let me die without despising you.
> Amurat's sentence does not stretch to her:
> Spare a life so little blest by fortune:
> Add this to all your other kindnesses;
> And if you ever loved me, madam . . .

ROXANE

> Go.

ACT FIVE, SCENE FIVE: *Roxane, Zatime*

ROXANE

> Traitor, you've seen Roxane for the last time:
> You go to face the punishment you've earned.

ZATIME

    Atalide prostrates herself to you
    And begs that you will hear her for a moment,
    Madam: she has a secret to confess
    Concerning you more closely than herself.


ROXANE

    Yes, let her come. You, follow Bajazet,
    And bring me word when he has met his fate.


ACT FIVE, SCENE SIX: *Roxane, Atalide*


ATALIDE

    I come no longer, madam, to pretend,
    Or trick the goodness I've so long abused;
    The stunned and worthy object of your hate,
    I come to you to bare my heart, and crime.
    I have deceived you, madam, it is true:
    Wholly consumed with my own love's concerns,
    My every thought when I saw Bajazet
    Was not to urge but to betray your cause.
    I loved him from my childhood; since that time
    Have shaped his feelings in a thousand ways.
    The sultaness his mother, blind to fate,
    United us and sowed the seeds of grief.
    You loved him since: you had been happier
    If you had seen my heart, or hidden yours,
    And known your love could not place trust in mine.
    I don't defame myself to clear his name:
    I swear by heaven, which sees me in disgrace,
    By my great ancestors the Ottomans,
    Who speak to you with me, on bended knee,
    For that unsullied blood we have from them.
    The prince in time had come to feel your grace,

Was not insensible to your appeal.
Jealous, ever prompt to emphasise
All that I thought fit to change his mind,
I left no course untried – tears, rage, complaints –
At times invoked his mother's royal shade,
This very day, most terrible of days,
Reproached him for the hope he'd given you,
And saying he must answer for my death
Did not relent in my unwelcome zeal
Until I'd wrung from him that pledge of faith
That was to seal his fate as well as mine.
But why should your indulgence be used up?
Don't dwell upon his coldnesses gone by:
It's I who forced them on him. What I broke
Will soon rejoin when I'm no longer here.
Whatever punishment my crime incurs
Do not yourself command my lawful death,
Don't show yourself to his bewildered gaze
Covered in blood that your own hands have shed:
Spare the faint strength of a too tender heart.
You can let me be mistress of my fate,
My dying will be no less prompt for that.
Enjoy the happiness my death secures
And crown a hero who will cherish you.
I'll see to my death; you see to his life.
Go, madam, go: before you can return
I will have slain the rival to your love.

ROXANE
I don't deserve so great a sacrifice:
I know how to do justice to myself;
And far from separating you, I plan
To bind you to him in eternal bonds:
Soon you'll enjoy the lovely sight of him.
Get up. But what distresses my Zatime?

## ACT FIVE, SCENE SEVEN: *Roxane, Atalide, Zatime*

ZATIME
Madam, come, show yourself, or else henceforth
The rebel Acomat is master here:
The sultans' sacred dwelling is profaned,
His lawless friends have forced the palace doors.
Those of your slaves remaining are unsure
Whether he serves you or betrays your cause.

ROXANE
Ah traitors! I'll confound him – see, I run.
I charge you with my captive: guard her well.

## ACT FIVE, SCENE EIGHT: *Atalide, Zatime*

ATALIDE
Alas! for whom should my heart make its prayers?
I cannot see what course they're set upon.
If you feel any pity for our plights
I do not ask you, Zatime, to betray
Roxane, or what she has resolved, to me;
But give me word, I beg, of Bajazet.
You've seen him? Must I still fear for his life?

ZATIME
Madam, I cannot help but pity you.

ATALIDE
What? Has Roxane already sentenced him?

ZATIME
Madam, I'm sworn to total secrecy.

ATALIDE
  Wretch, only tell me if he's breathing still.

ZATIME
  My life's at stake: there's nothing I can say.

ATALIDE
  You go too far, cruel woman: end it all:
  Give her a surer sign of loyalty;
  Your silence breaks my heart: now strike it through,
  Unfeeling slave of one herself a slave,
  Dispatch the life she wants to seize from me:
  Show yourself fit to serve her, if you can.
  You hold me here in vain; at this late hour
  I have to see him, or to end my life.


## ACT FIVE, SCENE NINE: *Atalide, Acomat, Zatime*

ACOMAT
  Ah madam, where can I find Bajazet?
  What is he doing? Can he still be saved?
  I've scoured the harem; at the same time
  Half my brave friends have gone a separate way
  Under Osmin's courageous captaincy;
  The rest have followed me. At every turn
  My eyes see nothing but a trembling crowd
  Of slaves and women seeking their escape.

ATALIDE
  O I know less about his fate than you.
  She knows all.

ACOMAT

        Fear my wrathful justice, slave,
Say what you know.


ACT FIVE, SCENE TEN: *Atalide, Acomat,
Zatime, Zaire*


ZAIRE

            O madam!

ATALIDE

                   Well Zaire,
What is it?

ZAIRE

        Fear no more: your rival's dead.

ATALIDE

Roxane?

ZAIRE

        And what will startle you far more,
Orcan himself, Orcan has murdered her.

ATALIDE

Orcan!

ZAIRE

        No doubt the failure of his mission
Drove him to take another life instead.

ATALIDE

Just heaven, innocence has your support!
Bajazet lives: Vizier, quick, run to him.

ZAIRE
Hear what has happened from Osmin's own lips:
He saw it all.

ACT FIVE, SCENE ELEVEN: *Atalide, Acomat,
Osmin, Zaire*

ACOMAT
Her eyes were not deceived?
Roxane is dead?

OSMIN
I saw the murderer
Withdraw the smoking dagger from her breast.
Orcan devised a cruel stratagem:
He served her only to secure her death;
For Amurat had charged him secretly
To murder first one lover then the other.
When Orcan saw us coming from afar,
He cried, 'Adore the order of your king.
Acknowledge his supernal signature.
Begone, you traitors, from this sacred house.'
He left Roxane expiring as he spoke
And strode towards us; in his bloody hand
He held the sultan's order, which enjoined
This monster to his double homicide.
We did not wait to hear him further, sir,
And borne away with anger and with grief
We punished his foul crime, and in his blood
Avenged at once the death of Bajazet.

ATALIDE
Bajazet!

ACOMAT
> What's that?

OSMIN
> > Bajazet is dead.
> You did not know?

ATALIDE
> > O heavens!

OSMIN
> > > Roxane, run wild,
> Fearing your coming, sir, outside this room
> Ordained the fatal noose should end his days.
> Myself I've seen the grimmest of all things,
> And sought in vain some sign that he still lived;
> But Bajazet was dead. We came on him
> Surrounded nobly by the dead and dying
> Who'd felt his vengeance but outnumbered him
> And now are the outriders of his ghost.
> That's done, sir: now we'd best look to ourselves.

ACOMAT
> O hostile fates, what have you brought me to?
> I know what you have lost in Bajazet,
> Madam; I know that in your present state
> It ill behoves me to pledge the support
> Of wretches who placed all their hope in him.
> Despairing, shattered by his crushing death,
> I will not look to save this guilty head
> But mindful of the needs of my sad friends
> Defend the lives they gave me to the end.
> You, madam, must decide if you'll entrust
> That sacred head of yours to other lands:
> We will effect it: masters of this place,

My faithful friends will wait to do your will;
Now I, to lose no precious moment more,
Must run to where my presence is required;
And where the sea laps at the palace walls
My vessels wait: I'll come to find you there.


ACT FIVE, SCENE TWELVE: *Atalide, Zaire*


ATALIDE
At last it's over: and by my deceit,
My fatal whims and my unfounded doubts
I have arrived at that unhappy pass
Of seeing my love pay for my own crime.
Fierce destiny, were you not satisfied
When you condemned me to outlive him here?
Why must you top my griefs by showing me
It was my love alone that caused his death?
Yes, it is I, sweet love, who take your life:
Not Roxane, and not Amurat, but I:
It's I alone who wove the sorry threads
That formed the hateful noose that stopped your breath.
And I can think of this and yet still live,
I who just now, when threatened with your death,
Fell faint, and let my fickle spirits flee.
Ah, was I only given love to kill?
Enough of this: by my prompt sacrifice
I'm punished and you're faithfully avenged.
And you, whose peace and glory I've defamed,
Heroes who should have lived again in him,
You too, unhappy mother, who from birth
Entrusted him to me with other hopes;
Ill-fated vizier, despairing friends,
Roxane – come all of you, conspire as one
To torture this distracted love-lorn girl

(*She kills herself.*)
   And take at last the vengeance due to you.

ZAIRE
   Ah, madam! . . . She has gone. O heaven, may I
   In this dark hour but share her grief and die!